Non-fiction  Level 1

# Things I do every day

by **Kate Riddle**

**PEARSON**

I wash my face
and hands.
What do I do next?

I brush my teeth.
What do I do next?

I comb my hair.
What do I do next?

I get dressed.
What do I do next?

I put my shoes on.
What do I do next?

I eat my breakfast.
What do I do next?

I go to school!